# BORN FOR
# SIGNIFICANCE

## STUDY GUIDE

# BORN FOR
# SIGNIFICANCE

## STUDY GUIDE

# BILL JOHNSON

CHARISMA
HOUSE

BORN FOR SIGNIFICANCE STUDY GUIDE by Bill Johnson
Published by Charisma House
Charisma Media/Charisma House Book Group
600 Rinehart Road, Lake Mary, Florida 32746

Visit the author's website at bjm.org, billjohnsonbooks.com.

Cataloging-in-Publication Data is on file with the Library of Congress.

International Standard Book Number: 978-1-63641-000-5

E-book ISBN: 978-1-63641-001-2

While the author has made every effort to provide accurate internet addresses at the time of publication, neither the publisher nor the author assumes any responsibility for errors or for changes that occur after publication. Further, the publisher does not have any control over and does not assume any responsibility for author or third-party websites or their content.

21 22 23 24 25 — 9 8 7 6 5 4 3 2 1

Printed in the United States of America

# CONTENTS

# PREFACE

**H**ELLO!
   I want to personally thank you for diving deeper into the book *Born for Significance* through this study guide. I believe the Lord is passionate about empowering His children to walk in their heavenly destiny, and I can't wait to see how He prepares you to live in yours as we learn and grow together through the content you're about to engage with.

When God first began speaking to me about the topic of living with significance, I had a sense that He wanted to move beyond praying for an upgrade and instead address matters of the heart. You see, everything in God's kingdom is a heart issue. That's what it means to move from one degree of glory to another: as He blesses us, He also refines us and strengthens us to carry the weight of our promotion. And our heavenly Father does it all in love, in the context of relationship with Him.

Through these eight sessions we'll explore the

BORN FOR SIGNIFICANCE STUDY GUIDE

scriptural basis that reveals God's heart for promoting His sons and daughters. You'll gain practical tools for taking hold of your next blessing and strategies for overcoming opposition along the way. You'll also glean fresh insight on how to use your blessing the way God intended—to bless others and glorify Him. In all of it I believe you'll grow in love for the Lord and His perfect design for humanity!

I'll be praying that as we walk through these sessions together, you will fall more in love with the One who created you and, along the way, begin to walk in the destiny He dreamed up for you at the beginning of time. Now is the time to live with the significance for which you were born!

Many blessings to you in your journey! I can't wait to hear about all the ways He's going to bless you as you step out in faith.

# HOW TO USE THIS STUDY GUIDE

I N ORDER TO prepare yourself to foster revival in your community, you need reinforcement. The keys that Pastor Bill Johnson provides in *Born for Significance* and in this corresponding study guide are designed for practical application in your daily life. Each of the eight interactive sessions in this study guide covers a chapter or chapters of the corresponding book. The study guide is designed to work best if you read the book's chapters first and then complete the questions in the study guide. Doing both will help you fully participate.

- **Individual study:** If you are working through this study on your own, you will

need the book *Born for Significance.* As
you read the related chapters in the book
and then answer the questions in each
of the eight interactive sessions, ask God
to speak to you and transform you. Keep
a Bible handy as well. Take your time
as you go through the material, and be
honest as you respond. Allow the Holy
Spirit to free you as you grasp a new
understanding of the significance you
were created for.

- **Bible studies and small groups:** If you
are a leader, have everyone obtain a copy
of *Born for Significance* and this study
guide. Refer to the facilitator's guide in
appendix A for instructions on how to
prepare, lead, and activate your group in
each session.

In each session there is an optional video viewing
guide. This will be of help to you if you are participating
in the video e-course created for this message. You can
learn more about the e-course at billjohnsonbooks.com.
If you are not participating in the e-course, simply
skip the video viewing guide and move on to the next
portion of each session.

In the exercises, you will have journaling space

following each of the questions. As you engage in each of the exercises, we pray that you will encounter the supernatural power of God and that you will continue to be transformed by the Holy Spirit as a growing disciple who learns how to recognize that you are born for significance!

# PURPOSE OF RULING

R EAD CHAPTER 1 of *Born for Significance.*
God designed you with a purpose, and one part
of that purpose is to grow. As you encounter Him in
greater degrees of intimacy, He promises to move you
from one degree of glory to another so that you might
look more and more like Jesus. That's His job as your
heavenly Father. Our role as children is to be faithful
in the transition from one degree of glory to the next
that we might be equipped to carry the full weight of
the blessings He has in store for us.

He promises an outcome of blessing, but that doesn't
mean the journey will be easy or even painless. Just
as Jesus suffered on the road to His destiny, we will
encounter trials on the path to ours. But the journey
toward glory is always worth the fight. It's when we

learn to say a joyful, faith-filled yes to the Father—even in moments of doubt and strain—that we can contain the great blessing He's releasing.

God's heart is to promote His sons and daughters so that we might walk in the significance He has called us to and, as a result, that we might display His glory to the nations. But attaining our great blessing isn't always as simple as desiring it in the first place. In His perfect design and plan the Lord works within a relationship-based protocol that ensures we can properly walk in the upgrades He has for us.

In this first session of the *Born for Significance Study Guide* you'll learn about the Lord's desire to bless and promote you and why it's a heavenly desire to advance in your God-given purpose. You'll also gain new insight on why it's so important to take hold of your destiny the way He intended and on how your obedience to Him blesses you, the people around you, and, most importantly, the Lord Himself. Are you ready to begin living in God's perfect design for your life?

## TO RULE AND TO SERVE

When God created the world, He always had relationship in mind. He desired to rule the earth with us, His sons and daughters, from the very beginning. If ever you feel without purpose, remind yourself of this powerful truth: we have the extraordinary privilege as His trusted, Spirit-filled children to live a life of eternal significance as we partner with Him in His purpose to rule and subdue the earth.

Before we can effectively walk in our God-given significance, we need a deeper understanding of the ways of His kingdom. First, we need to grasp our purpose as corulers. Every government in the world has two primary roles: to rule and to serve. When God blesses us to live out our heavenly destiny, it is not so that we might look good or feel important. Instead, He imparts blessing to us so we can make earth look like heaven!

## DISCUSSION QUESTIONS

1. How is our pursuit of kingdom blessing counter to the earthly pursuit of riches and material blessings?

2. What does it mean that we are called to *rule like servants but serve like kings*—and how does this approach empower us to make earth look like heaven?

3. Jesus is our perfect example of what it means to rule and serve. Can you think

of an example in Scripture where Jesus
does both of those things to display the
heart of God?

4. Our government is designed to protect
and empower. How can we protect and
empower others as we begin to walk out
our heavenly calling?

## SEEK FIRST HIS KINGDOM

When it comes to the pursuit of promotion, our priori-
ties matter. It's God's desire that we relentlessly, pas-
sionately pursue His heart above all else. Any fruit
that comes from our relationship with and obedience
to Him is an add-on. The beautiful thing is, as we
follow and encounter Him, we will also begin to see
a greater degree of blessing in our lives. Another way
to put it: When we give attention to what matters to
God, He gives attention to what matters to us.

The Lord has a divine purpose in wrapping up our
destiny in our relationship with Him: He wants us
to have the tools and resources we need to carry our
blessings well. Starting with our relationship builds a
firm foundation on which He can build a container for

everything He wants to release in our lives. Let's take a deeper look at how this plays out.

## DISCUSSION QUESTIONS

1. What happens if you build something on a shaky foundation?

2. Knowing this basic law of physics, why is it so gracious that God requires a solid foundation on which to build our blessing?

3. What does it mean that, along with God's kingdom, we're called to pursue His *righteousness*?

4. What does it say about the Lord that He teaches, refines, and advances us all in the context of relationship?

## VIDEO LISTENING GUIDE (OPTIONAL)

1. Everything that has to do
   with the kingdom of God is a

   _____.

2. Our ability to _____ nations
   depends on how well we _____
   from glory to glory.

3. We are called to rule with the heart of a
   _____ and serve with the heart of
   a _____.

4. Matthew 6:33 says, "Seek first His
   _____ and His _____, and
   all these things will be added to you."

5. You are perfectly designed for

   _____.

## ACTIVATION: BLESSED TO BE A BLESSING

In many circles it's common to adopt a posture of false
humility about pursuing blessings, which results in
missing out on opportunities to be a living display of
God's love and glory to other people.

Take time before the Lord to reflect on the next
promotion He wants to release to you. Ask Him how
you can use that blessing—whether it's a promotion
at work, a financial upgrade, or even physical or emotional healing—to bless other people.

As you pray and journal, ask the Lord to show you those He wants you to protect and empower as you walk out your blessing, as well as how your faithfulness could allow others to encounter Him in a new way.

Whenever you pray for the release of a promotion in your life, picture these individuals so that you can continue to steward God's design as you move from one degree of glory to the next. You were made to receive and share blessing, and He's preparing your next promotion today!

# JOURNAL

You're doing great so far! Let's move on to session 2 and continue learning about the significance God has for each one of us.

# POSITIONING YOUR HEART

R EAD CHAPTERS 2–3 of *Born for Significance*.
As you uncovered in the first session, God desires to build your significance on a healthy foundation, which means the process of becoming like Jesus is a vital part of attaining your blessings. One of the most important ways the Lord prepares you for advancement is by building your character. When you become more like Jesus in your heart, you can also begin to walk more fully in His power and influence.

While it's God's role to shape you into the person He has designed you to be, it's your role to steward your heart and, along the way, manage your thoughts, emotions, and actions. And as you position your heart toward the Lord and His desires, you will inherit—and beautifully steward—all the blessings He has prepared for you.

In many ways the state of your heart is a prophecy about your life. If your heart is connected to God and in tune with the way He's moving, you'll follow Him into your destiny. If, on the other hand, you're disconnected and tuned out, you won't get very far in living out your purpose. That's why Proverbs 4:23 instructs us, "Watch over your heart with all diligence, for from it flow the springs of life."

In this second session of the *Born for Significance Study Guide*, Pastor Bill introduces one of the most vital ingredients of advancement in the kingdom: growing in character. As you learn about the importance of aligning your heart and life with heaven, you'll be empowered to take bold steps toward your next promotion.

## ABIDING IN THE LORD

As you learned in the previous session, relationship is the primary context in which God readies us for our heavenly purpose. It's when we pursue His heart that we'll learn how to manage ours, which is a core component of showing the Lord we can be trusted with a promotion.

The first and foremost method for managing the well-being of our hearts is to abide in Jesus. Here's how it works: When we pursue His presence and encounter His heart in the process, we'll be transformed from the inside out. And when we become like Him on a heart level, we'll also be empowered to contain and carry the blessings He longs to unveil in our lives.

Let's take a deeper look at what it means to abide in Christ and how the pursuit of His presence can prepare us to carry all that He wants to release to us.

## DISCUSSION QUESTIONS

1. John chapter 15 introduces the concept of abiding in the Lord using the vine and branches analogy. How does this picture explain what it means to abide in God?

2. Abiding in Jesus helps us see God's heart. Why is this revelation so important if we want to *live* like Him?

3. How does abiding in Christ equip and empower us to pray for and prophesy His dreams and desires for us?

4. What does it mean that *we owe God
answers to prayer*? How does this principle fit in with abiding in Him and the
resulting release of our blessing in Him?

## THE PROBLEM WITH FALSE HUMILITY

As Pastor Bill explained, we can so easily fall into a
trap of false humility, where we decline an upgrade
because we think pursuing God's blessing is self-cen-
tered. The problem is, false humility is just as much
an act of disobedience as greed and materialism. And
both ways of living can be major barriers in Jesus'
command to bring the gospel to the nations.

Let's explore why it's so important to follow God
where He's calling us and how following Him toward
a greater degree of glory can lead us into both richer
blessing and a deeper dependence on Him.

## DISCUSSION QUESTIONS

1. Paradoxically, recognizing that God
wants to bless us and empower us can be
an act of humility. How can this be true?

2. Why is false humility an act of distrust,
   just as greed and materialism are?

3. How can your promotion enrich the lives
   of others and even show them the gospel?

4. After learning what you did in this
   week's session, what's the true definition
   of *humility*?

## VIDEO LISTENING GUIDE (OPTIONAL)

1. Your character is your _____.

2. God never gives up the _____ to say
   no to a request that will _____
   my purpose.

3. We owe God _____ to
   _____.

4. _____ is how you enter into
   God's protocol for promotion.

5. If you _____ yourself, He will
   _____ you at the right time.

## ACTIVATION: BEARING SPIRITUAL FRUIT

You learned in this week's session that abiding in God's presence is one of the most powerful ways to prepare your heart to live out His dreams for you.

To activate this lesson, prepare your heart to spend 15–20 minutes in God's presence. As you gaze upon the Lord, ask Him to reveal a character trait He wants to emphasize to you in this season.

Whether you journal or simply pray, make note of this character trait and how He might want to grow it in you. Pay special attention in your everyday life to this character trait, and look for opportunities to practice it.

For example, perhaps God revealed He wants you to grow in the spiritual fruit of patience. Be on the lookout for tangible opportunities to practice patience in situations in which you'd normally struggle, and watch as He faithfully makes you more like Him.

As you grow in His character, you're building a strong foundation for God to unleash the blessings of heaven in your life!

## JOURNAL

You did it! You made it through the second week. We're so expectant that God will continue to work in your life as we move forward. Let's go!

# PRINCIPLES OF PROMOTION

R EAD CHAPTERS 6–7 of *Born for Significance*.
In His great love the Lord longs to give you the desires and dreams of your heart so you can fulfill His design for your life. But as we've explored in the previous couple of sessions, He also wants us to be ready to carry our destinies. Only when we show we can be trusted to bear the weight of this great gift will He unleash the fullness of all that He has planned for our lives.

It may seem as if the Lord is somehow withholding His goodness from you, especially if you're watching someone else advance to the place you thought you were called to. But bitterness and jealousy will only serve as barriers from your personal calling. When you position your heart to value another person's journey toward success, choosing to honor the person's advancement, your act of obedience also sets you up for your own promotion.

We all have dreams burning in our hearts—seeds of desire planted by the Lord Himself, which when mature will bear eternal fruit in our lives and the lives of others. But as with any natural process, seeing these dreams bear mature fruit requires a specific set of steps determined by God. It's when we partner with Him in the principles of promotion that we will see His design for our lives unfold, one step at a time.

In this week's session you'll discover three of the primary principles of promotion and how God uses them to advance you toward your destiny. You'll also learn the significance of honoring others in establishing trust with the Lord and the reason it's so important to invite the Lord on your journey toward purpose.

## THEMES OF PROMOTION

We see it in Scripture, and we see it every moment of our lives. Our God, the Creator of all things, is a master designer. But it's not only our physical world that the Lord perfectly designed. He also perfectly created the ways of the kingdom—and we have a powerful opportunity to align ourselves with Him to live out these heavenly principles.

One way we can stay in step with God's creative

process is by aligning ourselves with Him as we pursue promotion. As you learned in this session, God relies on a specific set of principles to guide us toward our purpose in Him. Let's take a closer look at the principles of promotion and how they play out in our path toward spiritual significance.

## DISCUSSION QUESTIONS

1. In this session Pastor Bill shares that wisdom isn't just about finding solutions to problems. It's also a profound prophetic gift. How is wisdom prophetic?

2. One of the principles of promotion Pastor Bill introduces is excellence. How can excelling in your gifts position you for promotion? (Hint: Look up Proverbs 22:29.)

3. Creativity is another core component of moving forward in promotion. How can our creativity reflect the Lord to the world around us?

4. The last principle is integrity, or living with wisdom even when it costs you. Why is it so important that wisdom comes with sacrifice?

## HONORING OTHERS

As we learned in this session, we have a mandate to honor others by recognizing and celebrating their blessings. That means we sometimes have to overcome barriers, such as jealousy or bitterness, to honor. The beautiful thing is, when we choose to love even when it doesn't come naturally, we're also preparing ourselves for a greater measure of glory in our lives.

To finish up this week's discussion, let's examine the principle of honor and how it can refine us to contain the blessings God wants to release in our lives.

## DISCUSSION QUESTIONS

1. How is promotion an act of justice in God's eyes?

2. How does our refusal to honor another person's promotion war against God's justice?

3. How is flattery different from true honor?

4. What does it mean that *your honor sets the measure for what you can receive*?

5. Finally, why is it so important that we consider the state of our hearts when we bring correction to someone?

## VIDEO LISTENING GUIDE (OPTIONAL)

1. Promotion is an act of _____ in God's eyes.

2. God openly _____ the one who prays in _____.

3. Promotion always includes _____ and _____.

4. _____ is the counterfeit of honor.

5. If it doesn't hurt you to bring _____, don't do it.

## ACTIVATION: CHOOSING TO HONOR OTHERS

When we make the decision to honor others in their advancement, we obey God's command to love others as we love ourselves. In the process, we also show God we can handle the responsibility of our own blessing.

Spend some time examining your heart's posture toward other people in your life. Is there anyone you've felt jealousy toward because they're advancing in an area you also feel called to?

Go before the Lord and confess the state of your heart toward this individual. Then ask Him to soften your heart in love that you might feel authentic joy for this person's journey toward advancement.

To practice this heart posture when it doesn't come naturally, get your journal and write out five to ten honor statements toward this individual that celebrate their journey and gifts.

Finally, ask God to bless this person as they use their promotion for His kingdom. Together we can display His glory to the world!

**JOURNAL**

God is up to something amazing as He prepares your heart for promotion! We can't wait to jump into next week's session with you.

# THE POWER OF BLESSING

R EAD CHAPTER 5 of *Born for Significance.*
Think about the blessing or promotion you've
been seeking. Did you know God longs for that even
more than you do? You have an invitation to a greater
measure of glory, but it's ultimately up to you whether
you will position your heart to receive it. Part of that
positioning is maintaining a posture of humility as
you move from one degree of glory to the next.

You see, God gives blessings to those He trusts.
Only when we display that we are ready for the greater
portion will He release it in our lives. Walk with
wisdom, keep your trust in the Father, and aim to live
like Jesus—and don't be surprised when your dreams
start to come true. With your heart aligned to His,
your appetite will be aligned too.

If you have the Holy Spirit inside of you, God has entrusted you with all the power and authority you need to move mountains. But the measure of glory you received when you trusted in Jesus doesn't remain stagnant. The Lord wants to continue blessing you with promotion toward your ultimate purpose—but as with any riches, this blessing requires great stewardship.

In this fourth session, you'll learn about the important role of stewardship in your pursuit of significance. As you learn how carrying reward with responsibility and joy reflects the heart of God to others, you'll also glean practical insights on how to steward your blessing well, with a heart that's continually dependent on Jesus.

## HUMILITY IN BLESSING

Whether you receive the promotion you've been longing for is ultimately dependent on the state of your heart. God is strategic. He's looking for trustworthy partners to carry out His plan for humanity. Practically, what does that mean? One way this plays out is God's invitation to humility. He longs that we might maintain a humble posture of heart even as we confidently approach the throne.

Put another way, God is the giver of all good gifts—but it's up to us to position our hearts in dependence on Him even as we increase. Are you ready to explore how your appetite to please God with your life can multiply your blessings?

## DISCUSSION QUESTIONS

1. Why is it so important to maintain dependence on God even as you experience increase in your life?

2. Opposition is one way we stay humble in our journey of promotion. Why do we often encounter more opposition when we begin to live out our heavenly purpose?

3. How is opposition like an income tax on our blessing?

4. Paradoxically, when we pursue earthly riches, we don't gain much. What is it that God wants us to pursue first, and how does He bless us in the process? (Hint: Think back to Matthew 6:33.)

## STEWARDING THE BLESSING

Choice is a crucial part of God's design. He didn't make us to be computers because He wants us to operate in freedom. This principle applies when we choose to follow Him, and it's also important when we are contending for promotion in our lives. We have to choose to do it God's way every step of the journey.

Fortunately, He doesn't leave us to our own devices. Let's explore together God's perfect design for stewardship and what it looks like in our lives.

## DISCUSSION QUESTIONS

1. God wants to bless us because He loves us—but liberty is a core component of love. What does Pastor Bill mean when he says *when there are no choices, there is no reward*?


2. What does Pastor Bill mean when he says we need to start letting the Father be a father, and how is this important when it comes to stewarding our blessing?

3. First Kings tells a beautiful story about Solomon's rise to royalty. What does it mean that God gave Solomon favor because He loves Israel?

4. How does this truth apply to our personal promotion, and what does this tell you about the heart behind God's desire for blessing?

5. According to Pastor Bill's teaching in this session, how can you tell that you're misusing favor?

## VIDEO LISTENING GUIDE (OPTIONAL)

1. God desires your _____ more than you do.

2. It's more _____ to embrace elevation than fake _____ and go your own way.

3. God gives to people He _____.

4. _____ makes everyday things
   no longer _____.

5. Your identity is _____ when
   you become a responsible steward of the
   favor on your life.

## ACTIVATION: PROPHESYING STEWARDSHIP

God gives to those He trusts. As He refines your
character to make you more like Jesus, He's also preparing you to properly steward the blessings He wants
to impart to you.

Take some time with the Lord and envision your
life when you're living out the dreams you've been contending for. How has your life changed? More importantly, how can you use this transformation to be
generous toward other people?

As you reflect on what it will be like to live out
God's dream of promotion, think of some practical
ways you can steward that gift, and ask God to prepare your heart in the process.

You're getting closer to the advancement you've been
longing for, and in the process you're becoming more
like your Creator!

## JOURNAL

Can you believe we're already halfway through? We're praying for you as we continue on!

# THE PROMISES OF GOD

R EAD CHAPTER 4 of *Born for Significance.*
God has wonderful plans for each one of us
to uniquely reflect His beauty and goodness to those
around us—and we are all hardwired to long for this
world-shifting significance. So what happens in diffi-
cult seasons, when this sense of purpose feels far off?
What do we do when we begin to doubt, losing hope
that God will come through to provide the promotion
we've contended for?

The Lord has given us His promises as powerful
reminders that He hasn't forgotten. Even when we
lose sight of what's ahead, even when we're tempted to
give in to hopelessness, He's working all things for our
good. The work to attain this promise has already been
done by Jesus on the cross. But that doesn't mean we

don't have a role to play in securing the fullness of our inheritance. The Father desires that we would partner with Him, speaking His promises into fruition, even when all feels lost.

If you have a relationship with Jesus, you already know that He is faithful. He always does what He sets out to do—that's part of what makes Him so beautiful and worthy of our worship. Still, just because God is trustworthy doesn't mean we'll always believe it. We have a mandate to manage our hearts, speaking the promises of God over ourselves and prophesying His dreams over our lives.

In this session we'll explore the promises of God and how they serve to strengthen and nourish us as we contend for the blessings ahead. You'll be reminded afresh of God's work in securing your divine inheritance and your unique role in claiming it as your own—and in the process you'll gain momentum on your road toward becoming the person you were always meant to be. Are you ready to learn more?

## WAGE GOOD WARFARE

We've already learned about God's perfect, relational plan for imparting blessing in our lives and how He is looking for partners He can trust to fulfill the Great Commission on earth until He returns. But have you ever thought of this co-laboring as warfare?

When we live out and declare the promises He's spoken over us, we're not just building our own faith or even just giving the Lord the worship He deserves. We're also playing a major role in bringing heaven to earth. By His perfect design we can do our part to unleash God's dreams for our lives simply by trusting Him to be who He says He is!

## DISCUSSION QUESTIONS

1. God loves to shower His children in promises—about Him, about us, and about our lives fulfilling His plan. What does this characteristic reveal about the Lord's heart?

2. God could simply hand over what we ask for, but often He asks us to fight for it. Why is this such an important part of the process?

3. How is contending for your promise an act of spiritual warfare?

4. While we are empowered to take hold of our heavenly inheritance, it ultimately belongs to God. How does this reality affect your heart's posture toward promotion?

## RECEIVING AND APPREHENDING

Participation is a requirement when it comes to taking hold of God's promises. But taking part in His plan looks different for different people, depending on the season they're walking through. For example, you might be an expert at fighting for a promise and need a bit of help resting in God's grace. The opposite might be true for another individual.

The point is, getting what you've contended for isn't a one-size-fits-all process. God's goal is to refine you in the journey. Let's explore why that's important.

## DISCUSSION QUESTIONS

1. If you had to guess, are you in a season when God is inviting you to apprehend your blessing or quietly trust in Him to move on your behalf? Why do you sense this?

2. What does it say about the Lord's heart and character that He divinely tailors the process of moving toward promotion for each one of His children?

3. How can your faithfulness in the journey of apprehending or trusting help prepare you for the promise, and how can what you learn help you steward your promotion to bless and reflect God's love to others?

4. What does it mean that *fire always falls on sacrifice*, and why do you think this truth is relevant when it comes to fulfilling your God-given desire for significance?

## VIDEO LISTENING GUIDE (OPTIONAL)

1. When God gives us a _____, He's revealing who He made us to be.

2. The obstacle between the promise and its fulfillment requires _____.

3. God isn't obligated to fulfill our

_____.

4. If the Lord leads you into a
_____, He'll also prepare you
to _____.

5. _____ always falls on
_____.

## ACTIVATION: CLAIMING YOUR PROMISES

God's promises are like fuel for the journey. When we claim them as true, we have the strength to move forward toward promotion.

Take some time on your own with the Lord and make a list of five to ten promises He has spoken over you during your spiritual journey. Maybe they're Bible verses, prophetic words, or other forms of encouragement you've received.

Spend fifteen to twenty minutes praying these promises into fruition, declaring them over yourself and telling the Lord you trust Him to fulfill them. Turn your heart to thanksgiving, praising God in advance for fulfilling what He has spoken.

Next time you begin to feel discouraged in your path toward the promise, go back to this list and remind yourself of the truth. The God we serve keeps His promises! He's preparing you now to take hold of them so you can fulfill your destiny for His glory.

## JOURNAL

You were destined for a life of significance! Let's move forward and see what the Lord has in store over the next few weeks of learning and growing together.

# PROMOTION AND ADVERSITY

R EAD CHAPTERS 8–9 of *Born for Significance.*
God's plans always trump the forces of darkness—nothing can interfere with His goodness unfolding in your life. Still, the enemy will do whatever he can to prevent you from carrying out the Lord's design. Why? Because he's threatened by what God has put inside of you! Just as Jesus encountered opposition in His life and ministry, you can expect to experience trials and tribulations as you move from one degree of glory to the next.

It's easy to grow discouraged or even veer off track in the process of pursuing a promise, especially when the promotion you're seeking feels more like a distant dream than an impending reality. But don't back down when things get hard. The presence of opposition means you're getting closer to the blessing God wants to release in your life.

God makes a lot of promises to us, but He never promised we would live a conflict-free life. All of us experience trials and tribulations on this side of heaven. Even Jesus faced opposition when He walked the earth, which is a sure sign that as we walk toward our God-given callings, we'll experience opposition as well. But God is a good Father, and when we choose to partner with Him, we can be confident nothing will go to waste.

In this session you'll learn about how God uses conflict to shape and strengthen you and how you can respond to opposition in a way that sets you up to take hold of your destiny. As you gain a deeper understanding of why conflict occurs in our lives, you'll gain strength and resilience to continue fighting for all that the Lord has for you.

## THE PURPOSE OF CONFLICT

God wants the best for us. It's not the Father's will that His children would experience pain or difficulty. God isn't powerless against the enemy, and He won't let our spiritual conflicts go to waste. In His goodness and wisdom, the Lord intentionally allows us to experience the opposition that comes our way to prepare us to carry and steward the blessings He wants to pour out in our lives.

Let's explore the powerful purpose of opposition so that we might be encouraged next time we face adversity in the journey toward promotion.

## DISCUSSION QUESTIONS

1. Why does blessing attract conflict?

2. How can the opposition we experience help us value the promises God has set before us?

3. God wants us to feed on His promises when we are in the midst of conflict. Think about the purpose of the physical food you eat. What does it do for your body, and how does it help you live?

4. Why is it so powerful to tell the Lord you trust Him when you're experiencing opposition?

## WISDOM IN CONFLICT

Freedom is our inheritance, as children of God. That means we always have a choice of how to respond, whether we're enjoying blessing or facing opposition. Not only does how we choose to respond set our destiny into motion; it also puts our character on display to the world. Choosing to react to opposition with discouragement and unbelief sends one message, while walking through conflict with wisdom and grace sends an entirely different one.

To wrap up this week's content, let's take a closer look at how God wants us to respond to conflict and how our reaction to opposition can either compromise or enhance our witness to the world.

## DISCUSSION QUESTIONS

1. If you choose to embrace God's promises even when they haven't come to fruition yet, what does that say about the Lord to people watching you?

2. On the other hand, what message are you sending if you lose hope when things get hard and painful?

3. What does it mean that we can attract what we focus on, and how does this apply to our response to conflict?

4. The Lord has unlimited strength to give you, but the enemy has limited strength to oppose. How does this change your outlook on handling opposition?

## VIDEO LISTENING GUIDE (OPTIONAL)

1. Don't _____ immediately when you experience _____.

2. The _____ He deposits in us attracts _____.

3. The Lord rewards us based on

   _____.

4. The dogs of doom _____ at the doors of your _____.

5. You decide what you want to _____ in your life.

## ACTIVATION: OPPOSITION AND YOUR DESTINY

Oftentimes things heat up as we get closer to our destiny in the Lord. But the presence of conflict doesn't mean it is time to give up. It means it is time to put on the armor of God and wage war for what He promised you.

Take some time with your journal and reflect on previous seasons of your life when you dealt with conflict, adversity, or trials. Instead of focusing on the dark times, think about the victories they were preparing you for. How did each period of conflict open up your life to a greater degree of glory?

Spend ten to fifteen minutes in prayer or worship, thanking the Lord for using conflict in your life to strengthen you for your promise.

If you grow discouraged as you contend for the promotion ahead, return to this journal entry and reflect on God's powerful purpose in allowing conflict before victory.

**JOURNAL**

You have all the tools you need to overcome conflict and walk in your God-given purpose! Keep going! Let's move on to session 7 together.

# THE PAIN AND POWER
# OF REJECTION

Read chapters 10 and 12 of *Born for Significance*. Rejection hurts. There's no way around it. Whether we experience disappointment, loss, criticism, or betrayal, the grief of being rejected can quickly begin to overshadow the hope of God's promises over your life.

But rejection isn't the end of the story. Instead, it's a profound opportunity to strengthen yourself in the Lord, preparing your heart and refining your character to bear the weight of God's incredible promises over your life. Don't lose hope. By continuing to minister truth to yourself through the trenches of pain, you're building a history with God that will launch you into your destiny.

Rejection can actually launch you into your purpose when you align your heart with the Lord to steward it. While approaching your losses and disappointments with wisdom won't necessarily reverse the pain you've experienced, with a bit of strategy you can actually empower yourself to grow into the person God designed you to be.

In this session you'll learn about four of the most common ways the Lord uses rejection to groom you for promotion and why it's so important to keep your eyes on His plans in the process. You'll also develop your own arsenal of practical strategies for ministering to yourself when you face rejection in your path toward fulfilling your God-given destiny.

## THE REFINING POWER OF REJECTION

The perception of rejection can be crippling, even holding you back from stepping forward in your destiny, if you allow it to. But as with any challenge you face, the Lord sees opportunity where you see adversity. By partnering with His purposes, you can emerge from disappointment, loss, and betrayal even closer to your heavenly purpose than you started.

If you're ready to move past the grief and gain a fresh perspective on His heart for you in rejection, let's go deeper together.

## DISCUSSION QUESTIONS

1. How does your ability to handle disappointment affect your ability to carry blessing?

2. Why does how you handle loss reflect how you will handle gain down the road?

3. The ability to withstand criticism is another important component of stewarding rejection. Why is how you approach praise such an important predictor of how you'll handle criticism?

4. Lastly, how does your response to betrayal prophesy your response to blessing?

## RENEWING YOUR MIND

Your mind is a battleground. Even if you don't realize it, there's a war happening in your thoughts. Why is it that our thoughts are so often under siege? The enemy knows that our thoughts impact our emotions, and our emotions ultimately shape our behavior. If he can keep us in a state of discouragement and distrust, we won't take the action necessary for moving forward in the kingdom.

On the other hand, reflecting on Jesus and His promises can cause us to become more like Him—and as a result, we'll catapult ourselves into the blessing we long for. Let's take a closer look at God's design for our minds.

## DISCUSSION QUESTIONS

1. Romans 12:2 mandates that we "be transformed by the renewing of [our minds]." What does this scripture tell you about the relationship between your thoughts and your life?

2. Why is it so important to look back at God's character in the past, whether in your own testimony, in Scripture, or in the life of another believer?

3. What are some practical ways you can anchor your mind in truth?

4. In this session Pastor Bill encourages us to thank God in advance for miracles and blessings we haven't experienced yet. Why does this practice play a role in renewing your mind and, on a broader level, bringing your destiny into being?

## VIDEO LISTENING GUIDE (OPTIONAL)

1. Difficulties can _____ our focus or _____ us.

2. Disappointment helps us maintain _____ of heart.

3. If you don't live by _____, you won't die by _____.

4. You can't fully come into your _____ unless you know how to _____ to yourself.

5. The _____ is your mind.

## ACTIVATION: PRACTICING SELF-MINISTRY

At certain points in our lives, God brings us other people to speak truth into our hearts and strengthen our trust in Him. Other times, He teaches us how to nourish our own hearts through prayer, worship, and meditating on His promises.

Take twenty to thirty minutes to practice ministering to your heart. Turn on worship music, open up your journal, and soak in the Lord's presence. Ask Him if there's anything He wants to say to you, or open up your Bible and see if any scriptures or promises stand out.

Write these things down and declare them over yourself as a practice to strengthen your soul to believe God's word.

Over the next few weeks get in the habit of ministering to your own heart that you might sharpen your sensitivity to His Spirit and guide yourself back to truth when you lose sight of it.

## JOURNAL

We are praying for you as you continue through the course! It's time to move on to session 8.

# THE PERILS OF BLESSING

READ CHAPTERS 11 and 13–14 of *Born for Significance*. From the beginning of time, God has had a unique, divine plan for your life. Jeremiah 29:11 reminds us of this truth: "'For I know the plans I have for you,' declares the LORD, 'plans to prosper you and not to harm you, plans to give you hope and a future'" (NIV).

But God is just as strategic as He is good. Practically, that means He is as concerned about our growth and well-being as He is with delighting us with the desires of our hearts. That's why we face opposition and conflict in the pursuit of blessing, and it is why God allows the momentary pain of rejection and disappointment. All of it adds up to a greater good: that we will be blessed people who look like Jesus.

Blessing is your inheritance as a child of God. The Father delights in meeting the deepest desires of your heart, but be prepared—as you obtain your God-given blessings, you'll also start to look a lot like Jesus! It's up to you to continue stewarding this gift so that you might continue to grow in His likeness and your purpose.

In this final session of *Born for Significance* you'll learn about the cost that comes with taking hold of your blessing and how to ensure you stay connected to God and His divine purpose as you walk out your promotion. Even when you finally step into the significance you've always dreamed of, don't neglect to stay connected to the Lord and His heart!

## KNOWING YOUR WEAKNESS

The obstacles aren't over once you have finally been promoted. The devil is determined to bring temptation into your life to keep you from the growth God wants for you. One way this might manifest is a focus on material things or worldly blessings over obedience that results from an ongoing connection with God's heart.

God is good, and He doesn't leave you to your own strength when it comes to resisting obstacles. Let's explore in greater depth how you can prevent yourself from falling prey to weakness.

## DISCUSSION QUESTIONS

1. Why is it so important to be aware of your personal weaknesses before you face temptation?

2. Pastor Bill describes a proverb that addresses the importance of putting a knife to your own throat when you sit with a ruler (Prov. 23:2). What does this verse mean, and how does it apply to your personal promotion?

3. Sometimes we might be tempted to hold our own gifts hostage. Why is merely protecting our blessing the worst thing we can do?

4. What does it mean to *stay functional* with what God has given you to use for His glory, and why is this so important?

## FROM GLORY TO GLORY

God's promise has come to fruition in your life! What a beautiful testament to His faithfulness. What's next? Just as the Lord is passionate about equipping you to live out your desires, He's passionate about empowering you for continued growth. That's why Scripture tells us He wants to move us from glory to glory!

Let's explore the mechanics of our ongoing growth in the Lord and how we can maintain our connection with Him even as we grow in our kingdom stature.

## DISCUSSION QUESTIONS

1. What does it say about the Lord that He's passionate about both our growth and our blessings?

2. What happens when we begin to pursue our blessing by works and not by grace?

3. Why is it so important to recognize that your identity isn't in your blessing but in God Himself?

4. What does it mean to pursue blessing from a place of security and confidence in the Lord?

## VIDEO LISTENING GUIDE (OPTIONAL)

1. We're wired to _____ blessing, but we need to know the _____ that comes with it.

2. The worst thing you can do with blessing is simply _____ it.

3. Your _____ is not in blessing but in God Himself.

4. Religious _____ infects our sense of _____ and _____.

5. God's blessings are to _____ us to be blessings to _____.

## ACTIVATION: PREPARING FOR THE PROMISE

Over the last eight weeks, you've gained some powerful tools for taking hold of God's promises over your life.

Take some time in the Lord's presence to reflect on your time over the past eight weeks. What stuck out to you? What dreams and desires did He ignite? What promises is He speaking over you?

Take time to write out a prayer that thanks God for His work over the last eight weeks, identifying what He did in your heart. Then write out five to ten declarations that focus on how you want to grow moving forward.

For example, if you sense the Lord is inviting you to rest in the work He's already done on your behalf, you could write, "I am secure in the finished work of Jesus." If you want to grow in boldness, you could write, "I am strong and courageous in the Lord."

No matter what you learned, you can be confident God is preparing you for the glory ahead! We can't wait to see what He does!

**JOURNAL**

Thank you so much for participating in the *Born for Significance Study Guide*. God is at work in you, and His promises over your life will bear powerful, life-changing fruit!

# FACILITATOR'S GUIDE

I WANT TO PERSONALLY thank you for leading a group in my new e-course, *Born for Significance*. We couldn't do it without you! I believe the Lord will minister powerfully to your group over the next eight weeks. As you lead your group members in their own journeys toward promotion, I pray you'll also encounter Him in a new, transforming way.

When God first began speaking to me about the topic of living with significance, I had a sense that He wanted to move beyond praying for an upgrade and instead address matters of the heart. You see, everything in God's kingdom is a heart issue. That's what it means to move from one degree of glory to another. As He blesses us, He also refines us and strengthens us to carry the weight of our promotion. And our heavenly Father does it all in love, in the context of relationship with Him.

Through our next eight weeks together, we'll explore the scriptural basis that reveals God's heart for promoting His sons and daughters. You'll gain practical tools for taking hold of your next blessing and strategies for overcoming opposition along the way. You'll also glean fresh insight on how to use it the way God intended—to bless others and glorify Him. In all of it I believe you'll grow in love for the Lord and His perfect design for humanity!

We designed this leader's guide, which is more than a workbook, to be an invaluable resource in leading others. We hope the insights that correspond with each week's video teachings not only prepare you for your meeting but encourage you as a leader. Every week includes a brief explanation of that week's teaching, along with key concepts and questions to inspire your group.

I'll be praying that as we walk through this course together, you fall more in love with the One who created you and, along the way, gain the tools you need to empower yourself and your group to walk in the Lord's dreams. Now is the time to live with the significance for which you were born!

MANY BLESSINGS,
BILL JOHNSON

## BASIC LEADER GUIDELINES

This study is designed to help you develop into a believer who can cultivate, sustain, and carry revival wherever you go. From *this* perspective, you will partner with God to see impossibilities bow at Jesus' name and will step into the destiny God has for you as you discover how you were born for significance.

As a leader, you'll be equipping your group to grow in their relationships, so it's important you feel equipped as well. Our goal is to empower you with all the tools you need so you can lead your group from a place of overflow.

Each week of the leader's guide contains two main sections: preparing and leading. In the preparing portion you'll have prompts and journaling space to engage with God about that week's topics. We have also included bullet points of potential conversation starters, should you need some help, including general concepts from the video teaching. Expect to spend about 30–45 minutes preparing for each session. We would recommend preparing a few days before your group. This way the material will stay fresh but you'll have time to hear from the Lord and process beforehand.

You can plan on meeting once a week as a group to watch the video, engage with the content, and activate what you've discussed and learned. Though meeting times can vary, depending on how talkative your group is, 60–90 minutes should leave plenty of time for God to speak to and encourage your group.

When all is said and done, this curriculum is unique in that the end goal is *not* information; it is transformation. The sessions are intentionally sequenced to take every believer on a journey from information to revelation to transformation. Participants will receive a greater understanding of what partnership with heaven looks like as they discover who they are in Christ and how to live a life of blessing and promotion.

We bless you on your journey with the *Born for Significance* e-course as you prepare and lead. Thank you again for your partnership in connecting those around you to Him and one another! We pray that as you go through this study, you will see the culture of your families and communities begin to look more and more like the culture of heaven.

## WEEKLY OVERVIEW OF GROUP SESSIONS

Here are instructions on how to use each of the weekly "Discussion Questions" guides.

### Welcome and Fellowship Time (10–15 Minutes)

This usually begins 5–10 minutes before the designated meeting time and continues up until 10 minutes after the official starting time. Community is important. One of the issues in many small group/class environments is the lack of connectivity among the people.

**Welcome:** Greet everyone as they walk in. If it is a small-group environment, as the host or leader, be intentional about connecting with each person as they enter the meeting space. If it is a church-class environment, it is still recommended that the leader connect with each participant.

**Refreshments and materials:** In the small group you can serve refreshments and facilitate fellowship among group members. In a class setting talk with the attendees and ensure that they have all their necessary materials (the workbook and a copy of *Born for Significance*). Ideally the small-group members will have received all their resources before session 1, but if not, ensure that the materials are present at the meeting and available for group members to pick up or purchase.

**Pray:** Open every session in prayer, specifically addressing the topic that you will be covering in the upcoming meeting time. Invite the presence of the Holy Spirit to come, move among the group members, and stir greater hunger in each participant to experience more of God's transformative love and power in their lives.

## Introductions (10 Minutes—first class only)

**Introduce yourself** and allow all participants to briefly introduce themselves. This should work fine for both small-group and class environments. In a small group you can go around the room and have people introduce themselves one at a time. In a classroom setting establish some type of flow, and then have each person give a quick introduction (name, interesting fact, etc.).

**Discuss** the schedule for the meetings. Provide participants an overview of what the next eight weeks will look like. If you plan to do any type of social activities, you might want to communicate this right up front.

## Worship (15 Minutes—optional for the first meeting)

Fifteen minutes is a solid time for a worship segment. That said, it all depends upon the culture of your group. If everyone is OK with doing 30 minutes of praise and worship, by all means go for it! For this particular curriculum a worship segment is highly recommended, as true and lasting transformation happens as we continually encounter God's presence.

## Prayer/Ministry Time (5–15 Minutes)

At this point you will transition from either welcome or worship into a time of prayer. Just like praise and worship, it is recommended that this initial time of prayer be 5–10 minutes in length, but if the group is made up of people who do not mind praying longer, it should not be discouraged. The key is stewarding everyone's time well while maintaining focus on the most important things at hand.

The prayer component is a time when group members will not just receive prayer but also learn how to exercise Jesus' authority in their own lives and witness breakthrough in their circumstances. After the door is opened through worship, the atmosphere is typically charged with God's presence.

**Transition Time**

At this point you will transition from prayer/ministry time to watching the *Born for Significance* videos.

**Video/Teaching (20–25 Minutes)**

During this time group members will answer the questions in their workbooks and have a place to take notes.

**Discussion Questions (20–30 Minutes)**

In the Leader's Guide there will be a number of questions to ask the group. Some questions will be phrased so you can ask them directly; others may have instructions or suggestions for how you can guide the discussion.

Some lessons will have more questions than others. Also, there might be some instances when you choose to cut out certain questions for the sake of time. This is entirely up to you, and in a circumstance when the Holy Spirit is moving and appears to be highlighting some questions more than others, flow in sync with the Holy Spirit. He will not steer you wrong!

As you ask the question in the group setting, encourage more than one person to provide an answer. Usually you will have some people who are off in their responses, but you will also have those who provide part of the correct answer.

Participants may feel as if the conversation was lively, the dialogue was insightful, and the meeting was an overall success, but when all is said and done, the question "What do I do next?" is not sufficiently answered. This is why every discussion time will be followed by an activation segment.

## Activation (5–10 Minutes)

- Each activation segment should be 5–10 minutes at the *minimum*, as this is the place where believers begin putting action to what they just learned.

- The activation segment will be custom tailored for the session covered.

- Even though every group member might not be able to participate in the activation exercise, it gives them a visual for what

it looks like to demonstrate the concept
they just studied.

## Plans for the Next Week (2 Minutes)

Be sure to let group members know if the meeting
location will change or differ from week to week, or
if there are any other relevant announcements to your
group/class. Weekly e-mails, Facebook updates, and
text messages are great tools to communicate with
your group. If your church has a database tool that
allows for communication between small-group/class
leaders and members, that is an effective avenue for
interaction as well.

## Close in Prayer

This is a good opportunity to ask for a volunteer to
conclude the meeting with prayer.

## SESSION 1: PURPOSE OF RULING

## Step 1: Prepare

*Reflect*

Review the following key concepts from Pastor Bill's
teaching this week to prepare your heart and mind to
lead. In the space below take some time to note the
ideas that stick out to you.

- Everything in the kingdom of God is a
  heart issue.

- God designed us to move from glory to glory, so we need to learn how to transition well.

- We must rule with the heart of a servant but serve with the heart of a king.

- The Lord wants us to use His blessings to bless the people around us.

- It's His goal to build something in you that can contain what He's releasing.

*Pause*

Listen to God's heart for this week. Spend time in prayer, asking the Lord what He wants to share with those in your group. Journal here what you hear. Make sure you include any ideas you have for your group time.

## Step 2: Lead

*Watch*

Start by watching the video from session 1. Suggest that group members take notes and write down what stands out to them, especially for use during the workbook homework.

*Discuss*

Spend time dialoguing about the video content, covering the key concepts and talking points you prepared. If you'd like, ask two or three of the following questions to stir conversation. Here are possible questions you could use:

- What does it mean that everything in the kingdom of God is a heart issue?

- What does Jesus' life on earth teach us about what it means to love others the way God intended?

- What is the protocol the Lord uses to promote us, and what does this say about His heart?

- What does it mean that God doesn't want to break us with a blessing?

- What's significant about the word *proverb*, and how does it apply in our journey toward promotion in the Lord?

- Why is it so important to submit to those who are ahead of us in their spiritual journey?

## Step 3: Activate

In many circles it's common to adopt a posture of false humility about pursuing blessings, which results in missing out on opportunities to be a living display of God's love and glory to other people.

Have your group members take time before the Lord to reflect on the next promotion He wants to release to them. Encourage them to ask Him how they can use that blessing—whether it's a promotion at work, a financial upgrade, or even physical or emotional healing—to bless other people.

As they pray and journal, tell your group members to ask the Lord to show them those He wants them to protect and empower as they walk out their blessing as well as how their faithfulness could allow others to encounter Him in a new way. Have them get in groups of two or three and share about what they journaled.

Lastly, encourage them that whenever they pray for the release of a promotion in their lives, they can picture these individuals.

Thank you for stepping out and leading your group into purpose and promotion!

## SESSION 2: POSITIONING YOUR HEART

### Step 1: Prepare

*Reflect*

Review the following key concepts from Pastor Bill's teaching this week to prepare your heart and mind to lead. Take time to journal through the ideas that stick out to you.

- "An inheritance gained hurriedly at the beginning will not be blessed in the end" (Prov. 20:21).

- Your character is your container.

- Faith brings answers, but enduring faith brings answers with character.

- He never gives up the right to say no to a request that will undermine my purpose.

- Personal significance positions us as people of God to disciple nations.

*Pause*

Listen to God's heart for this week. Spend time in prayer, asking the Lord what He wants to share with those in your group. Journal here what you hear. Make sure you include any ideas you have for your group time.

## Step 2: Lead

*Watch*

Start by watching the video from session 2. Suggest that group members take notes and write down what stands out to them, especially for use during the workbook homework.

*Discuss*

Spend some time dialoguing about the video content, covering the key concepts and talking points you prepared. Ask two or three questions to stir conversation. Here are possible questions you could use:

- What does it mean that all the issues of life come from the heart?

- Why won't an inheritance gained in a hurry be blessed?

- Why do you think God chooses to give us promotions through the journey of a relationship?

- What does it mean to abide in God, and how does it look practically?

- Why is loyalty such an important principle for promotion?

- What does the story of Daniel teach us about promotion and blessing?

## Step 3: Activate

Your group members learned in this week's session that abiding in God's presence is one of the most powerful ways to prepare their hearts to live out His dreams.

To activate this lesson, have your group members spend 15–20 minutes in God's presence, asking Him to reveal a character trait He wants to emphasize to them in this season.

Whether in a journal or prayer, have them make note of this character trait and how He might want to grow it in them. For example, maybe God is emphasizing patience. In this case someone could be on the lookout for tangible opportunities to practice patience in situations in which they would normally struggle.

Have each person in your group share the character trait to the group that the Lord showed them.

As your group members grow in His character, they are building a strong foundation for God to unleash the blessings of heaven in their lives!

God is doing powerful things in your life and the lives of your group! Now let's move on to session 3 together.

## SESSION 3: PRINCIPLES OF PROMOTION

### Step 1: Prepare

*Reflect*

Review the following key concepts from Pastor Bill's teaching this week to prepare your heart and mind to lead. Take time to journal through the ideas that stick out to you.

- It's hard to celebrate another person's promotion when they were called to the place we thought we were called to.

- When we get trapped in false humility and we don't accept promotions, we are actually warring against the justice of God.

- We have to live celebrating the sovereignty of God, so when He elevates one, we yield to it and give honor where it's due.

- In heaven everyone is valued for who they are without being stumbled over for who they are not.

- The army of Christ is the only army that kills their wounded.

*Pause*

Listen to God's heart for this week. Spend time in prayer, asking the Lord what He wants to share with those in your group. Journal here what you hear. Make sure you include any ideas you have for your group time.

## Step 2: Lead

*Watch*

Start by watching the video from session 3. Suggest that group members take notes and write down what stands out to them, especially for use during the workbook homework.

*Discuss*

Spend time dialoguing about the video content, covering the key concepts and talking points you prepared. Ask two or three questions to stir conversation. Here are possible questions you could use:

- How can false humility hold us back from promotion?

- Why is it so important to consider what happened "behind the scenes" of another person's blessing?

- What does it mean that wisdom is often the basis for promotion?

- What does it mean to know another person after the Spirit and not the flesh?

- Why is it so important that God extends an invitation to us to co-labor with Him rather than forcing us into it?

- What does it mean that we can *lock someone into failure*?

## Step 3: Activate

When we make the decision to honor others in their advancement, we obey God's command to love others as we love ourselves. In the process we also show God we can handle the responsibility of our own blessing.

Have your group members spend some time examining their hearts' posture toward others. Ask them if there is anyone they have felt jealousy or bitterness toward as they pursue their own promotion.

Next, encourage them to go before the Lord and confess the state of their heart toward this individual. Then tell your group members to ask Him to soften their hearts in love so they might feel authentic joy for this person's secret journey toward advancement.

To finish, tell your group to write out five to ten honor statements toward this individual that celebrate the person's journey and gifts, then to pray for increased blessing on this person.

Have them gather in groups of two to share. If they need to ask for forgiveness or forgive someone, have them commit to their partner a time frame in which that will happen.

Together we can display His glory to the world!

Ready for next week? We can't wait to dive back in with you!

## SESSION 4: THE POWER OF BLESSING

### Step 1: Prepare

*Reflect*

Review the following key concepts from Pastor Bill's teaching this week to prepare your heart and mind to lead. Take time to journal through the ideas that stick out to you.

- God desires your blessing more than you do.

- When you emphasize going without, you can't live out God's dreams for your life.

- It's a humbler choice to embrace elevation from God than fake humility.

- Through blessing we can develop an appetite for earthly things.

- God gave Solomon favor because He loves Israel.

- Wisdom makes everyday things no longer mundane.

*Pause*

Listen to God's heart for this week. Spend time in prayer, asking the Lord what He wants to share with those in your group. Journal here what you hear. Make sure you include any ideas you have for your group time.

## Step 2: Lead

*Watch*

Start by watching the video from session 4. Suggest that group members take notes and write down what stands out to them, especially for use during the workbook homework.

*Discuss*

Spend time dialoguing about the video content, covering the key concepts and talking points you prepared. Ask two or three questions to stir conversation. Here are possible questions you could use:

- What does it say about God's character that He longs for our blessing even more than we do?

- Why is it a humbler choice to accept a blessing rather than decline it?

- What does Jesus' life tell us about what we can expect on the path toward personal significance?

- Why do you think it's so easy to develop an appetite for earthly things when we are blessed?

- Why is it so important to say thank you and accept kind words when someone praises you?

- How is your identity enhanced when you steward the blessing on your life?

## Step 3: Activate

God gives to those He trusts. As He refines your character to make you more like Jesus, He's also preparing you to properly steward the blessings He wants to impart to you.

Encourage your group members to take some time with the Lord and envision their lives when they are living out their dreams. How has their life changed? More importantly, how can they use this transformation to be generous toward other people?

As they reflect on what it will be like to live out God's dream of promotion, have them think of some practical ways they can steward that gift, and encourage them to ask God to prepare their hearts in the process.

Have them gather in groups of two or three and share their dreams. Then have the groups pray into that vision.

You and your group are getting closer to the advancement you've been longing for, and in the process you're becoming more like your Creator!

You're doing so well! We can't wait to continue learning and growing with you.

## SESSION 5: THE PROMISES OF GOD

### Step 1: Prepare

*Reflect*

Review the following key concepts from Pastor Bill's teaching this week to prepare your heart and mind to lead. Take time to journal through the ideas that stick out to you.

- Promises define our destiny.

- When God gives a promise, it's like He goes into our future and comes back to us with a word that will help get us there.

- Everyone around you is approaching their advancement differently.

- We need both power and authority to carry out our purpose.

- Our deliverance is for other people to know what it is to be free.

- Fire always falls on sacrifice.

*Pause*

Listen to God's heart for this week. Spend time in prayer, asking the Lord what He wants to share with those in your group. Journal here what you hear. Make sure you include any ideas you have for your group time.

## Step 2: Lead

*Watch*

Start by watching the video from session 5. Suggest that group members take notes and write down what stands out to them, especially for use during the workbook homework.

*Discuss*

Spend time dialoguing about the video content, covering the key concepts and talking points you prepared. Ask two or three questions to stir conversation. Here are possible questions you could use:

- How do God's promises reveal what He made us to be?

- What does it mean to wage good warfare according to prophecies?

- Pastor Bill uses an illustration of a baby chick. What does this picture reveal about our process of fighting for blessing?

- What does it mean that God isn't obligated to fulfill our potential?

- What is the definition of an inheritance?

- Why does God allow us to experience conflict?

- Where does our spiritual power come from?

## Step 3: Activate

God's promises are like fuel for the journey. When we claim them as true, we have the strength to move forward toward promotion.

Tell your group to make a list of five to ten promises the Lord has spoken over them. Maybe they're Bible verses, prophetic words, or other forms of encouragement they have received.

Then encourage your group members to spend 15–20 minutes praying these promises into fruition in groups of three or four. Declare these declarations over each other.

Next time you and your group members begin to feel discouraged in your path toward the promise, go back to this list and remind yourself of the truth. The God we serve keeps His promises! He's preparing you now to take hold of them so you can fulfill your destiny for His glory.

Session 5 is complete! Let's move on to see what else the Lord wants to do in your group.

## SESSION 6: PROMOTION AND ADVERSITY

## Step 1: Prepare

*Reflect*

Review the following key concepts from Pastor Bill's teaching this week to prepare your heart and mind to lead. Take time to journal through the ideas that stick out to you.

- Don't put down the pursuit of blessings just because you've seen someone misuse it.

- The word God deposits in us attracts conflict.

- Sailors can advance against adverse wind.

- Not everyone is going to be as excited about your promises as you are.

- Sometimes we will be forced to learn how to celebrate someone else's breakthrough.

- A spirit of offense can poison our hope.

*Pause*

Listen to God's heart for this week. Spend time in prayer, asking the Lord what He wants to share with those in your group. Journal here what you hear. Make sure you include any ideas you have for your group time.

## Step 2: Lead

*Watch*

Start by watching the video from session 6. Suggest that group members take notes and write down what stands out to them, especially for use during the workbook homework.

*Discuss*

Spend time dialoguing about the video content, covering the key concepts and talking points you prepared. Ask two or three questions to stir conversation. Here are possible questions you could use:

- What does it mean that the Lord rewards us based on choices?

- Why is it so important to decree the Word when we are discouraged?

- Why can't we afford to have a thought in our minds that God doesn't have about us?

- Why does how we label our emotions or behaviors matter?

- Why is the enemy so bent on opposing believers pursuing promotion?

- Pastor Bill shared an illustration about a snake going up a mountain. What does this tell us about what the enemy can and can't do?

**Step 3: Activate**

Oftentimes things heat up as we get closer to our destiny in the Lord. But the presence of conflict doesn't mean it is time to give up. It means it is time to put on the armor of God and wage war for what He promised you.

Have your group members take some time with their journals and reflect on previous seasons of their lives when they dealt with conflict, adversity, or trials. Instead of focusing on the dark times, tell them to think about the victories they were preparing them for. How did each period of conflict open up your group members' lives to a greater degree of glory?

Finally, have your group spend 10–15 minutes in prayer or worship, thanking the Lord for using conflict for strengthening. Encourage them to return to this journal entry and reflect on God's powerful purpose in allowing conflict before victory.

Are you ready for our next week together? Let's keep up the momentum!

## SESSION 7: THE PAIN AND POWER OF REJECTION

### Step 1: Prepare

*Reflect*

Review the following key concepts from Pastor Bill's teaching this week to prepare your heart and mind to lead. Take some time to journal through the ideas that stick out to you.

- Difficulty can strengthen your focus or destroy you.

- If it happened to Jesus, we have to assume it will happen to us. The servant is not greater than the Master.

- You can't come into your destiny fully until you know how to minister to yourself.

- Fear of man encourages us to embrace an inferior lifestyle.

- The battleground is your mind.

*Pause*

Listen to God's heart for this week. Spend time in prayer, asking the Lord what He wants to share with those in your group. Journal here what you hear. Make sure you include any ideas you have for your group time.

## Step 2: Lead

*Watch*

Start by watching the video from session 7. Suggest that group members take notes and write down what stands out to them, especially for use during the workbook homework.

*Discuss*

Spend time dialoguing about the video content, covering the key concepts and talking points you prepared. Ask two or three questions to stir conversation. Here are possible questions you could use:

- How does the Lord groom us through rejection?

- Why should praise be like a supplement (but not food)?

- What does the story of Jesus tell us about how rejection works in our lives?

- What does it mean to anchor your soul in God's decree over your life?

- What role does worship play in your promotion?

- What role do godly friendships play in the process?

## Step 3: Activate

At certain points in our lives God brings us other people to speak truth into our hearts and strengthen our trust in Him. Other times, He teaches us how to nourish our own hearts through prayer, worship, and meditating on His promises.

Have your group members take 20–30 minutes to practice ministering to themselves, asking the Lord if there's anything He wants to say or opening up the Bible to look for encouraging scriptures. Encourage them to write these things down and declare them as an anchoring strategy.

Encourage your group members to get in the habit of ministering to their own hearts that they might guide themselves back to truth.

We have one more week together to learn about transitioning to a greater measure of glory! Let's prepare our hearts expectantly to hear from God.

## SESSION 8: THE PERILS OF BLESSING

### Step 1: Prepare

*Reflect*

Review the following key concepts from Pastor Bill's teaching this week to prepare your heart and mind to lead. Take some time to journal through the ideas that stick out to you.

- We're wired to pursue blessing, but we need to know the cost.

- You sacrifice favor when you start wanting someone else's stuff.

- Your sacrifice and thankfulness should be equal to the miracle you received.

- Reformers by nature are living for another generation.

- We can't reduce our walk merely to retain a blessing; we have to keep it moving forward.

- The Lord sometimes withdraws His presence not to punish us but to make clear what's in our hearts.

*Pause*

Listen to God's heart for this week. Spend time in prayer, asking the Lord what He wants to share with those in your group. Journal here what you hear. Make sure you include any ideas you have for your group time.

## Step 2: Lead

*Watch*

Start by watching the video from session 8. Suggest that group members take notes and write down what stands out to them, especially for use during the workbook homework.

*Discuss*

Spend time dialoguing about the video content, covering the key concepts and talking points you prepared. Ask two or three questions to stir conversation. Here are possible questions you could use:

- What does it mean that blessings come with a cost?

- How do we sacrifice favor when we want what someone else has?

- Why is it so important that our thankfulness is the same measure as our miracle?

- Why is it so dangerous when worship becomes a formula?

- What does the story of Hezekiah teach us about handling promotion?

- What does it mean to make decisions out of our identity in Christ?

## Step 3: Activate

Over the last eight weeks you and your group have gained some powerful tools for taking hold of God's promises.

Have your group gather in groups of three or four to reflect on your time in this e-course. What stuck out in the teachings? What dreams and desires did He ignite? What promises is He speaking? Next, have them share testimonies or breakthroughs that happened.

Then tell them to individually write out five to ten declarations that focus on how they want to grow moving forward.

For example, if one person senses the Lord is inviting them to rest in the work He's already done, they could write, "I am secure in the finished work of Jesus." If they want to grow in boldness, they could write, "I am strong and courageous in the Lord."

No matter what your group learned, each one of you

can be confident that God is preparing you for the glory ahead! We can't wait to see what He does!

End your final session together in worship, thanking God for who He is and all He did over the past eight weeks.

Thank you so much for participating in the *Born for Significance Study Guide*. God is at work in your group, and His promises over your lives will bear powerful, life-changing fruit!

# VIDEO SESSION ANSWER KEY

## Session 1: Purpose of Ruling

1. Heart issue

2. Disciple, transition

3. Servant, king

4. Kingdom, righteousness

5. Obedience

## Session 2: Positioning Your Heart

1. Container

2. Right, undermine

3. Answers, prayer

4. Loyalty

5. Humble, exalt

## Session 3: Principles of Promotion

1. Justice

2. Honors, secret

3. Blessing, responsibility

4. Flattery

5. Correction

## Session 4: The Power of Blessing

1. Blessing

2. Humble, humility

3. Trusts

4. Wisdom, mundane

5. Enhanced

## Session 5: The Promises of God

1. Promise

2. Participation

3. Potential

4. Conflict, win

5. Fire, sacrifice

## Session 6: Promotion and Adversity

1. Stumble, adversity

2. Word, conflict

3. Choices

4. Bark, destiny

5. Attract

## Session 7: The Pain and Power of Rejection

1. Strengthen, destroy

2. Humility

3. Praise, criticism

4. Destiny, minister

5. Battlefield

## Session 8: The Perils of Blessing

1. Pursue, cost

2. Protect

3. Identity

4. Routine, passion, identity

5. Enable, others

# NOTES